BABY ANIMALS

BABY CHEETAHS

Martha E. H. Rustad

a Capstone company — publishers for children

Raintree is an imprint of Capstone Global Library Limited, a company incorporated in England and Wales having its registered office at 264 Banbury Road, Oxford, OX2 7DY – Registered company number: 6695582

www.raintree.co.uk
myorders@raintree.co.uk

Hardback edition © Capstone Global Library Limited 2022
Paperback edition © Capstone Global Library Limited 2023
The moral rights of the proprietor have been asserted.

All rights reserved. No part of this publication may be reproduced in any form or by any means (including photocopying or storing it in any medium by electronic means and whether or not transiently or incidentally to some other use of this publication) without the written permission of the copyright owner, except in accordance with the provisions of the Copyright, Designs and Patents Act 1988 or under the terms of a licence issued by the Copyright Licensing Agency, 5th Floor, Shackleton House, 4 Battle Bridge Lane, London SE1 2HX (www.cla.co.uk). Applications for the copyright owner's written permission should be addressed to the publisher.

Edited by Alison Deering
Designed by Jennifer Bergstrom
Original illustrations © Capstone Global Library Limited 2022
Picture research by Tracy Cummins
Production by Tori Abraham
Originated by Capstone Global Library Ltd

978 1 3982 2381 3 (hardback)
978 1 3982 2382 0 (paperback)

British Library Cataloguing in Publication Data
A full catalogue record for this book is available from the British Library.

Acknowledgements
We would like to thank the following for permission to reproduce photographs: Newscom: Suzi Eszterhas/Minden Pictures, 12; Shutterstock: Alexey Osokin, 5, 6, Chris Fouri, 11, Eric Isselee, back cover, gd_project, 21 top, Louise Victor, 13, Maggy Meyer, 9, Manny DaCunha, 20 top, Mary Ann McDonald, 7, nwdph, 17, 19, oksana2010, 20 bottom, Paul Tessier, 14, Stu Porter, cover, 15, 18.

Every effort has been made to contact copyright holders of material reproduced in this book. Any omissions will be rectified in subsequent printings if notice is given to the publisher.

All the internet addresses (URLs) given in this book were valid at the time of going to press. However, due to the dynamic nature of the internet, some addresses may have changed, or sites may have changed or ceased to exist since publication. While the author and publisher regret any inconvenience this may cause readers, no responsibility for any such changes can be accepted by either the author or the publisher.

Printed and bound in India

Contents

Newborn cheetahs 4
Sights and sounds 8
Eating and hunting 12
Growing up! 16
    Run like a cheetah 20
    Glossary 22
    Find out more 23
    Index 24

Words in **bold** are in the glossary.

NEWBORN CHEETAHS

Look! There are new babies on the African **savanna**. These babies are cheetah **cubs**. Cheetahs are part of the cat family.

Cheetah cubs grow inside the mother for three months. Mother cheetahs give birth to **litters** of three to five cubs. Each cub weighs about 0.5 kilograms (1 pound). The mother licks her cubs clean.

The mother cheetah keeps her cubs in a nest in tall grasses. This hides them from **predators**. Every few days, she moves them to a new nest. She gently picks each cub up by the folds of skin on its neck.

A mother cheetah raises her cubs by herself. Newborn cubs are blind and helpless. Their mother's strong eyesight looks for danger.

SIGHTS AND SOUNDS

Adult cheetahs are brown with black spots. But baby cheetahs have fuzzy silver fur on their backs. This keeps them hidden in tall grasses. It also helps the cub stay cool in hot weather.

Cheetahs make lots of sounds. But they do not roar. They snarl, hiss and grunt at predators. Mother cheetahs purr.

Hungry cubs mew and squeak. They also chirp. Chirps help mothers and cubs find each other if they are apart.

EATING AND HUNTING

When they are born, baby cheetahs drink milk from their mother. By 6 weeks old, they have teeth. This means they can eat meat.

A mother cheetah hunts **prey** daily. She takes meat to her cubs. Cheetahs hunt animals such as **antelope**, rabbits or other small **mammals**.

After about two months, cheetah cubs start to follow their mother. She teaches her cubs to hunt. The cubs watch their mother closely. She sneaks up on prey. She creeps closer. Then she runs fast!

Cheetahs are the fastest animals on land. They can run up to 97 kilometres (60 miles) per hour. But they can only run that fast for 20 to 30 seconds.

When she catches prey, a mother cheetah calls her cubs to eat. Their tiny, sharp teeth rip and chew meat.

GROWING UP!

Cheetah cubs play with their brothers and sisters as they grow. They sneak up on each other. They **pounce** and chase. They practise their hunting skills. Soon they will start to hunt small animals.

Young cheetahs need lots of hunting practice. At first, they cannot catch much. They still need help from their mother to survive.

17

Cheetahs are fully grown by the age of two. They are ready to leave their mother. They can take care of themselves.

Some adult cheetahs live alone. Male cheetahs often live with their brothers. Female cheetahs have cubs at about the age of three. Cheetahs live for about 12 years.

RUN LIKE A CHEETAH

Cheetahs can run very fast for about 30 seconds. In that time, they travel about 500 metres (1,600 feet). How far can you run in 30 seconds?

What you need

- a ruler or tape measure
- tape or chalk
- a stopwatch

What you do

1. Find a friend or adult to be your helper.
2. Mark a starting line. Ask your helper to time you.
3. When your helper says "go", run as fast as you can for 30 seconds.
4. Measure how far you ran.

How far did you run?

Did you run as far as a cheetah?

Glossary

antelope animal that looks like a large deer and runs very fast

cub young animal that eats meat

litter young born to an animal from the same pregnancy

mammal warm-blooded animal that breathes air; mammals have hair or fur; female mammals feed milk to their young

pounce jump on something suddenly and grab it

predator animal that hunts other animals for food

prey animal that is hunted or killed by another animal for food

savanna open lands with grasses and short shrubs

Find out more

Books

Big Cats (DKFindout!), DK (DK Children, 2019)

Cheetahs (Animals), Jaclyn Jaycox (Raintree, 2021)

Cheetahs (Nature's Children), Cynthia Unwin (C. Press/ F. Watts Trade, 2019)

Websites

www.bbc.co.uk/cbbc/watch/deadly-60-steve-races-a-cheetah
Watch Steve Backshall race against a cheetah on the CBBC website!

www.dkfindout.com/uk/animals-and-nature/cats/cheetah/
Learn more about cheetahs with DKFindout!

Index

adulthood 18–19

African savanna 4

appearance 8

birth 4

diet 12–13, 15

eyesight 7

habitat 4, 6, 8

hunting 13, 14–15, 16

lifespan 19

litter 4

playing 16

predator 6

prey 13, 14–15, 16

siblings 4, 16, 19

sounds 10

speed 14–15

weight 4